Spot the Difference

Leaves

Charlotte Guillain

Heinemann LIBRARY

www.heinemann.co.uk/library
Visit our website to find out more information about Heinemann Library books.

To order:
 Phone 44 (0) 1865 888066
 Send a fax to 44 (0) 1865 314091
 Visit the Heinemann Bookshop at www.heinemann.co.uk/library to browse our catalogue and order online.

First published in Great Britain by Heinemann Library, Halley Court, Jordan Hill, Oxford OX2 8EJ, part of Harcourt Education. Heinemann is a registered trademark of Harcourt Education Ltd.

© Harcourt Education Ltd 2008
The moral right of the proprietor has been asserted.

Editorial: Sian Smith and Cassie Mayer
Design: Joanna Hinton-Malivoire
Picture research: Erica Martin and Hannah Taylor
Production: Duncan Gilbert

Printed and bound in China by South China Printing Co. Ltd

ISBN 978 0 431 19230 7

12 11 10 09 08
10 9 8 7 6 5 4 3 2 1

British Library Cataloguing in Publication Data
Guillain, Charlotte
  Leaves. - (Spot the difference)
  1. Leaves - Juvenile literature
  I. Title
  581.4'8

Acknowledgements
The publishers would like to thank the following for permission to reproduce photographs: ©FLPA pp.**12**, **22 left**, **23a** (Keith Rushforth), **15**, **23c** (Krystyna Szulecka), **8**, **23b** (M. Szadzuik / R. Zinck), **13**, **23d** (Martin B Withers), **5**, **6** (Nigel Cattlin); ©istockphoto.com pp.**4 bottom right** (Stan Rohrer), **4 top left** (CHEN PING-HUNG), **4 top right** (John Pitcher), **4 bottom left** (Vladimir Ivanov); ©Jonathan Buckley p.**21** (flowerphotos.com); ©Photolibrary pp.**11**, **17**, **18**, **20**, **22 right** (Botanica), **16** (Creatas), **7** (Ifa-Bilderteam Gmbh), **14** (J S Sira), **9** (Kit Young), **19** (Mark Bolton); ©Science Photo Library p.**10** (Bjanka Kadic).

Cover photograph of beech leaves reproduced with permission of ©FLPA (Nigel Cattlin). Back cover photograph of a Swiss cheese plant reproduced with permission of ©FLPA (M. Szadzuik / R. Zinck).

Every effort has been made to contact copyright holders of any material reproduced in this book. Any omissions will be rectified in subsequent printings if notice is given to the publishers.

Contents

What are plants?

Plants are living things.
Plants live in many places.

Plants need air to grow.
Plants need water to grow.
Plants need sunlight to grow.

What are leaves?

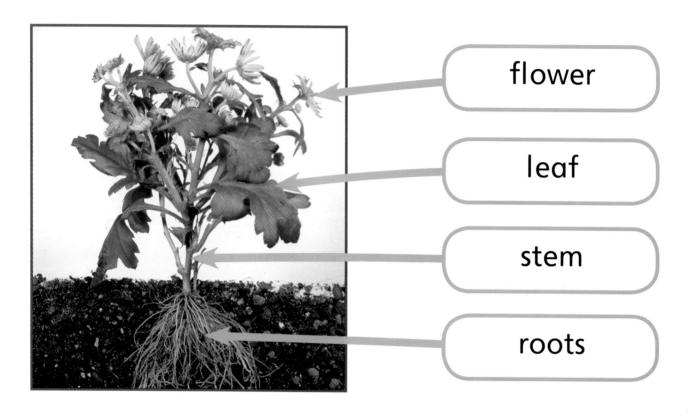

flower

leaf

stem

roots

Plants have many parts.
A leaf is a part of a plant.

Most plants have leaves.

Different leaves

This is a Swiss cheese plant.
Its leaves are smooth.

This is a pussy ears plant.
Its leaves are hairy.

This is a tulip.
It has few leaves.

This is a fern.
It has many leaves.

This is a pine tree.
Its leaves are narrow.

This is a banana plant.
Its leaves are wide.

Amazing leaves

This is a living stone plant.
Its leaves are soft.

This is a monkey puzzle tree.
Its leaves are spiky.

This is a yucca plant.
Its leaves are very long.

This is a water lily.
Its leaves are very round.

This is a flame nettle.
Its leaves are red.

This is an ivy plant.
Its leaves are yellow.

What do leaves do?

Leaves use sunshine to make plant food.

Leaves help plants grow.

Spot the difference!

How many differences can you see?

Picture glossary

 **narrow** close together

 **smooth** flat; does not have bumps

 **spiky** has sharp points

 **wide** far apart

Index

Notes to parents and teachers

Before reading

Take in a collection of different leaves from trees and plants. Talk to the children about the different shapes and sizes. Can anyone tell you what trees the leaves came from? Ask the children to tell you some of the differences between the leaves, for example, large or small, rough or smooth, hairy or prickly.

After reading

- Tell the children you are going to quiz them about things they heard in the book. Ask them: Do most plants have leaves or do most plants not have leaves? Are all leaves the same shape? Are all leaves the same colour? Are all the leaves prickly? How do leaves help the plants?
- Give each child an outline of a leaf made from thin card, for example; an oak, sycamore, holly, or beech leaf shape. Ask them to draw around their template and then to cut out the leaves they have drawn. Help them to stick these onto an appropriate tree outline that you have drawn. Write the name of the tree (using a yellow highlighter) and ask the children to go over your word to label the leaves.
- Tell the children that they are going to sway like the leaves on a tree. Select a piece of music (or use a CD of 'wind') and tell the children they should sway with the wind. Ask them to use their hands as if they were the leaves blowing in the wind. Vary the strength of the wind so that they have to move more quickly or slowly.